Black Mom Magic:
How to Use What You Got to Get What You Want

Neoshi Green-Kebreau

Neoshi Green-Kebreau
Black Mom Magic: How to Use What You Got to Get What You Want
Loxahatchee, Florida

Copyright © 2016 Neoshi Green-Kebreau. All rights reserved. No part of this publication may be reproduced, stored in or introduced into a retrieval system, or transmitted, in any form or by any means (electronic, mechanical, photocopying, recording or otherwise), without the prior written permission of the copyright owner.

The scanning, uploading, and distribution of this book via the Internet or via any other means without the authorization of the publisher is illegal and punishable by law. Please purchase only authorized electronic editions and do not participate in or encourage electronic piracy of copyright materials. Your support of the author's rights is appreciated.

Editor: Robin Devonish, Self-Publishing Maven
2nd Editor/Proofreader: Candice Briggs, EA Writing Services
Layout: Robin Devonish, Self-Publishing Maven
Formatting: Istvan Szabo, Ifj, Sapphire Guardian Publishing

ISBN 13: 978-0-9982873-6-2
ISBN 10: 0-9982873-6-9

Printed in the United States of America

Acknowledgements

Special thanks to my parents Ike & Betty Green
for always believing in me and my vision.

My husband, Hubert Kebreau Jr.,
thank you for all of your love and support.

To my children, Nyasia and Allahkheem,
thank you for choosing me.

My amazing in-laws, Hubert & Odile Kebreau,
thank you for all of your love.

To my mentor Lucinda Cross-Otiti,
I feel blessed to call you a friend.

To all of my extended family and friends
thank you for always being my cheerleaders.

WE DID IT!

Contents

Foreword (Written by Hubert Kebreau Jr.)..................................5

Introduction..8

Chapter 1: That's My Story & I'm Sticking to It.............................13

Chapter 2: Are Those Your Shoes or Did You Borrow Them?..19

Chapter 3: No Queen Left Behind..30

Chapter 4: Bag Lady Tendencies...34

Chapter 5: Put Some Respect On It 41

Chapter 6: Chick Don't Kill My Vibe 53

About the Author..59

Foreword
Written by Hubert Kebreau Jr.

Well, to say the least, my wife Neoshi definitely has that Black Mom Magic. When she told me the title of her book I thought to myself, "That sounds a little raunchy and ratchet, like a ghetto Queen B." But I know she isn't that type of woman. In fact, when I look back over the past 15 years we've been together, she's always done just what this book is about. Neoshi used what she had to get what she wanted or where she needed to be in a respectful way and was always in pursuit of her destiny.

I remember in college when we met back in 2001 we had the same chemistry class; she was a pharmacy major and I was studying Opticianry. Now for the love of me, I couldn't understand anything the professor was talking about, period! So, I found myself in the back of the class looking at all the pretty girls. "Which one to pick?", I said to myself. Then I spotted her. This dark chocolate, sun-kissed, honey succulent (sorry, got carried away with my flashback). I spotted her sitting in the front row looking all attentive, taking notes wearing big, nerdy, round, 1980 glasses but she! Looked! GOOD!

The next day after class I waited outside on a bench next to the classroom door for her to come out. When she did, I played it off and was like, "You're in this Chemistry class with Mr. (whatever his name was) Right?" She replied "Yes," and the rest was history. Now even though I failed that chemistry course, I did succeed in making her my girl. Now back to the point.

When we spoke, we would talk about our future and what we wanted to achieve. At that time Neoshi was working at a local pharmacy and would often complain about how the people came in like drug addicts screaming, passing out and trying to sell their babies for medication (well not really but the way she described it, that may have been the next step). She said she wanted to help people in a real way in bettering their lives. She didn't know exactly how but after those experiences she knew becoming a pharmacist wasn't it.

I was in my second year of college and didn't know totally and truly what I wanted to do yet. For Neoshi, however, she had already begun to break the spell of following money to happiness. You know what I'm talking about – The career advice people give you when you don't know what you want to do. "Do what makes you money," they say. She broke that spell her first year of college. Instead, she wanted to do what made her happy. She stayed in that job for a few more years but had already begun looking for something more fulfilling.

Fast forward to early 2007, when we found out she was pregnant with our first child. She quit her job as a pharmacy technician and set out on a journey to do more and be more. From there, slowly but surely she adjusted her lens of intuition and tweaked her path closer and closer to her heart's calling.

She started a side hustle that became a full-fledged 6 figure business in 2 years, created a blog that featured interviews with successful business women and celebrities, hosted her own events and conference, and launched her magazine, all in less than four years. I was amazed (and I still am) at her dedication and perseverance no matter how tough things were at times.

Sometimes I would get upset and say, "you spent money on what?!" Now I always supported her, but when you're working in a line of work that's tiring you don't want money to go so quickly. However, she has always operated on the principle of abundance.

No doubt, Neoshi has mastered the secrets to using what you got to get what you want. The tips in this book, however, are a testament to the magic found in each and every one of us. Our magic is a God-given way to help us move mountains. It's a positive energy that only works for the goodness of life.

Take heed to the words in this book. It's straight to the point and a quick read so you can hurry up and get your life together.

INTRODUCTION

As women, I think we've become accustomed to using our sexuality to get what we want. We're known to bat our eyes, throw a little smile and sometimes use sex to get what we want. Yes, the power of our vagina is real, but it's not the only power we possess. As women we have been blessed with certain "superpowers," if you will, that men aren't so lucky to have. Not only are we able to grow whole human beings inside of us, but our bodies also equip us with everything we need to nurture and support them. From our ability to produce the perfect milk made just for our babies, our ability to multitask, to our magical intuitive powers as well. In fact, the powers that we possess are enough to change the entire course of the human race. We are goddesses. We are blessed with the power to manipulate the future through the very thing that crowns us as women - our children. Through their interaction with us, they learn and are affected by our thoughts, words and actions. Now tell me that's not powerful!

As a mom of 2, I have seen first-hand the magnitude of a mother's influence on her children. My children teach me things about myself that I never understood and they reveal parts of me I never knew existed. They motivate me to do better so I can show them better. I've learned that children will not just do as you say, but they also watch what you do. As moms we're quick to tell children what they need to do, but rarely do we take our own advice. We tell them just to be themselves and not care what anyone thinks, yet we're breaking our backs to impress people we don't even know or like. We tell them to go after your dreams and don't let anyone or anything stop you, yet we're in a job we hate and in relationships that don't make us happy. We have to start practicing what we preach! Not just for our children but ourselves as well. Let me ask you this: Do you want to be happy? Do you want to feel fulfilled? Don't you think you deserve to be happy and fulfilled?

As children, we dream freely and often, but as adults, we think dreams are just that, dreams. If we don't accomplish what we want by a certain age, we immediately tell ourselves it's never going to happen. In doing that, we allow our life challenges to become our life crutches. As a woman who has done this myself, I've also witnessed other women do the same thing, especially black women and black moms in particular. As moms we automatically put our needs on the back burner and when you couple this with the challenges we face, the results can be crippling. Stop a random mom on the street and ask her what she wants most. Then ask her why she isn't going after it. Her response will be the same as every other mom on the planet - Lack. Lack of time, money, or help! And those responses are why Black Mom Magic was birthed.

The truth is we lack time because we devote it to the wrong things and people. We lack money because we invest it in the wrong things. In fact most of us don't invest we just spend it on things to make us feel better and mask the pain and frustration we're feeling. And sadly enough, we lack help because we're forced into situations that are either out of our hands or due to bad decisions. Divorce, incarceration, and entertaining the wrong men have left a lot of black women single and handling the workload of two. Even with a spouse or partner, shit gets real when you have children to raise and bills to pay. With so much on your plate you don't even want to think about anything else that looks or smells like work. That's why so many of us have given up on our dreams and goals. And if it involves money forget about it. They're not trying to see money get "wasted on something that may never work out anyway". We have completely given up. Where is the fight? Where is the determination? What ever happened to, "where there is a will, there is a way." What happened to the magic? Yeah we love to scream "Black Girl Magic!" but most of us haven't used ours in decades. It's time to dig her up, dust her off and really begin to work your magic. Your magic is the unique and divine ability to take the hand you've been dealt and turn it into something profound and beautiful.

Black Mom Magic: How to Use What You Got to Get What You Want provides real life solutions to create the change you want to see in your life. Every day we lecture our children about doing something great with their lives, yet most of us aren't leading with the example to show them firsthand. In this book, you'll learn powerful tricks to get what you what every single time despite time, money, or mommy duties. You'll also have the opportunity to test out your magic skills as I walk you through simple yet powerful 'Work Your Magic' exercises that help you make immediate changes to your life and the way you see it.

"Our blood reeks of royalty they can smell it in the air. We're so used to our own scent we cannot fathom what we bear."
–Korryn Gaines

Chapter 1
That's My Story & I'm Sticking to It

As a child, I was teased a lot about my dark complexion. They say the darker the berry, the sweeter the juice, but that's not how I saw it at all. To me, my dark skin was a curse and I hated it. Although my parents told me I was beautiful all the time, the words mean nothing to a child who doesn't hear it from their peers.

I had extremely low self-esteem, which affected my confidence and how I showed up in the world. Often the quiet girl in the corner, I envied the light-skinned girls in school and rarely spoke up for myself. It wasn't until I met my now husband in college, that my perception of self, changed.

He treated me like a queen, told me I was a queen and made me feel like one. He helped me change how I saw myself and how I felt about myself. He told me that I was beautiful and the darkness of my complexion was a blessing.

Now I've had boyfriends while in middle school, high school and college, but I'd never heard that from any of them. Hearing it from Hubert was life changing. But he didn't just tell me; he showed me.

He spoke with so much conviction that I felt stupid for doubting my beauty in the first place. I immediately began to make up for lost time and begin a new path to self-love. I stopped telling myself that I was too black or wasn't pretty enough. And I stopped doing things that devalued my worth.

Trick: Change your thoughts because your thoughts reinforce your beliefs.

Some of us look at our story as what happened to us. But it's so much more than that. Your story is a combination of your challenges, how you overcame and how it shaped your life. Your story can empower you or devour you. You see, a devouring story will hold you back, but an empowering story will push you forward. To see the empowering side of your story you have to understand what your mindset was at that time and why you chose to make the decisions you made.

Where were you mentally?

Were you "young and dumb"?

We're you in a sticky situation that left you between a rock and a hard place?

In hindsight, what is your understanding of the situation now?

What did you learn from that experience and how has it made you a stronger person?

When you can see the experience at its core, then you're able to see how it's shaped you for the better and the changes you've made to your life as a result of that experience. That is where your power lies. Here's an example:

Devouring Story: I got pregnant my freshman year in college and couldn't finish school. Now I'm stuck working two jobs just to get by while I try to finish my degree in night school.

Empowering Story: As an adopted child I often struggled with my identity and made stupid decisions trying to fit in. I had unprotected sex in college and got pregnant during my freshman year. Initially, I was devastated, but my daughter is the best thing that's ever happened to me. Instead of giving up, I decided to work two jobs and go to school part-time so I could complete my degree in Psychotherapy.

Trick: Eliminate negative stories you've created about yourself and create new ones that support you.

Your story can make you or break you. It's not what's in your story so much that affects your life. It's how you respond to and react to the elements of your story.

So what's the story you've been telling yourself? How can you turn it around to empower yourself and your situation so that you can move forward? Everyone has a sad story about their life and all the hell they went through, but never let it define you nor confine you.

"Whatever we believe about ourselves and our ability comes true for us."

– Susan L. Taylor

Work Your Magic:
List three devouring stories you've been telling yourself then rewrite them so that they become empowering stories.

Devouring story #1
_____
_____
_____
_____

Re-write that story, so it now becomes Empowering:
_____
_____
_____
_____
_____

Devouring story #2:
_____
_____
_____
_____

Re-write that story, so it now becomes Empowering:
_____
_____
_____
_____
_____

Devouring story #3:

_____
_____
_____
_____
_____

Re-write that story, so it now becomes Empowering:

_____
_____
_____
_____
_____

"Greatness is not measured by what a man or woman accomplishes, but by the opposition he or she has overcome to reach his goals."
–Dorothy Height

You were divinely designed to handle everything and every obstacle that comes your way. Kill your pity party whenever things don't happen the way you intended. Don't complain and walk around with a "woe is me" attitude focusing on everything that's wrong in your life and feeling sorry for yourself. You can't stay in this zone and be happy. The two don't mix! Problems don't get solved in this zone! Especially all of the issues you can't seem to stop complaining about on a regular basis.

Change your thoughts, change your beliefs and change your negative stories about yourself. In doing this, you've gained a deeper awareness and understanding of the factors in your life. Now you're empowered to restructure your life and move toward what you truly desire.

Chapter 2
Are Those Your Shoes or Did You Borrow Them?

If you're like most people, you've got a million and one ideas about how to make money or get ahead in some way. But of all those ideas, how many have you carried out? I'm willing to bet not many (no shade). And it's because of all the excuses we make as to why we can't do it and why it simply won't work. Let's not deny it. Let's be real. I'm woman enough to own up to it and so should you. And although I make a conscious effort not to, I still fall victim to not executing an idea, more times than I'd like to admit.

But why does this happen? Is it because we don't have the time or resources? Or because it wasn't meant to be? We can't do it all, right? WRONG! As I stated in the introduction, most, if not all moms, will state **lack** as the number one reason for not being where she wants to be. Again, the lack is in time, money or resources due to obligations of her mommy duties. The lack, however, is a ***perceived lack***. It's not real. What you perceive as lack is a flawed and conditioned pattern of thinking which consistently seeks and produces a reason to keep you where you are. "But I don't want to stay where I am and why would I do that?" you ask. Most often the answer is fear or discomfort. Stepping outside of your familiar surroundings and into uncharted territory can be terrifying. Therefore, to avoid the fear or discomfort, you (without even thinking about it) create a false pretense that you're **lacking** something instead of recognizing the internal power within to create or generate the resources, time or money you claim you don't have.

Trick: Get Rid of Self-Imposed Roadblocks & Think Outside of the Box.

Yes, I know the kids are a handful, and yes I know your money only spreads so far. However, experience has taught me that if you want something bad enough you will get it. Not only will you figure out a way to make it happen, but you won't give up until it happens. Excuses are road blocks that say I don't want to go there, I'm afraid to go there or I'm just not interested. It's important to know the source of your road blocks. Sometimes we allow other people to set road blocks for us and we don't even know it. It can be friends, family or even society. Of the three, society is the most dangerous because our daily surroundings have a way of ingraining themselves into our everyday thoughts and actions. If society says we should walk, talk or act a certain way, then we try to walk that line, so we don't look crazy. We think we have to do things a certain way because that's the way "they" say things should be done. And, I believe, it's the reason why many people are walking around unhappy and frustrated. Trying to fit in, be something we're not and trying to walk in someone else's shoes. Busy looking at what everybody else is doing and how they're doing it that you lose yourself. Forget everybody else! What do you want? Learn to think outside of the box and go beyond the "normal." Doing this not only opens you up to the possibilities of life but also helps you destroy the "lack" mentality. The more you practice open minded thinking, the easier it will be to see the resources, time or money needed to get what you want.

Trick: Start Where You Are.

When all else fails, start where you are. That means doing what you can with what you already have. Again, it may require you taking the path less traveled or creating a new one based on what you're working with. Moving from 'where you are' puts you in the habit of beginning somewhere, anywhere, instead of sitting around trying to "figure things out." As you move, you will see what works and what doesn't. You'll also begin to discover if it's what you want. It's easy to say you want something when you don't have it, but it's another thing to experience it and decide it's not what you expected and you'd feel fine living without it. Experience is invaluable, and by starting where you are, you can begin to weed out the unwanted on the road to your goals.

Trick: Trust Your Intuition.

Some people call it a voice, some people call it a feeling, but it's a very useful tool. Even when it doesn't make sense, you have to trust your intuition. It can seem like something so little or insignificant, but in hindsight, you will realize it wasn't. I remember telling this to a room full of children once and a friend shared a perfect example which had happened to her just that morning. She said she was driving along and "something," told her not to take the highway and to take the local street instead. And of course, she was in a rush and said to herself if I take the local road it's going to take me twice as long to get there. Although it made no sense, she knew from experience that she should listen and took the local road as instructed.

After driving a few more miles, she hears a strange sound then realizes her tire had popped. She slowly pulled over to the side of the road and after the usual dammit, shit and every other curse word we say during a time like that, she immediately realized why "something" told her to take the local roads. She said, "Imagine if I had been driving on that highway at sixty plus miles an hour and my tire popped. Things could have been a lot worse." Your intuition is there not only to guide you to where you need to be, but also to protect you from what you don't see.

My most memorable experience with my intuition was in 2010 when I got the wake-up call of my life. I had just landed a job at an AT&T call center and was excited about the possibilities for moving up in the company. Previous to this I had been applying for jobs in management with other companies but never made it past the initial interview. So when my cousin told me about the call center and that they were looking for management, I became excited. I remember looking around the room on my first day and getting this little nudge and the little voice that said, you're not supposed to be here. And I thought to myself, "I'm definitely not supposed to be in this room as a call representative. I'm supposed to be in management that's for sure." You see, I've always known I would have my own business and that if I had to work for anyone it would have to be in a position where I had more freedom and less restriction like management. However, I brushed the feeling off and decided to make the best of the opportunity.

A few weeks later, I was sitting in another training session and I heard the same voice again, but this time it was much louder. And it repeated the same thing as before, "you're not supposed to be here." This time, the voice resonated with me much more because earlier that morning my husband was urging me to quit. He was concerned about our schedules and not having me around as much as he'd like with the children. He asked me to consider staying at home with the children and allow him to take care of us financially. Now, most women I know would have jumped at that opportunity immediately, but I took pride in being able to provide for my family financially and did not want to let go of that. Again, this voice and the feeling that came with it was not taking no for an answer. A few days later I called the company and told them that I decided to resign and would not be returning. Upon hanging up, I immediately felt a sense of relief although I was nervous about not being able to contribute financially. So at the advice of my husband (and my intuition co-signing) I decided to sell herbal weight loss products as a side hustle to bring in extra money. I knew they would sell because of how well they worked on me but didn't realize how quickly it would change my life. After just one year I had made so much money that I was forced to incorporate as a registered business. And the year after that my business had grown to six figures annually. Not only was I making five times more than I would have made if I'd stayed at that call center, but I was also running my own business; something I always knew was part of my destiny. Now every day I get to stay at home with my children and do what I love. Trust your intuition; it will never let you down.

"I did what my conscience told me to do, and you can't fail if you do that."

–Anita Hill

Work Your Magic:
Think of a problem you've been wrestling with for a while now.

Problem:

_____
_____
_____
_____
_____

Now stop and intensively listen. What is your intuition telling you to do about it?

_____
_____
_____
_____
_____

Trick: Talk Less, Bubble More.

Everybody knows a Talking Tammy. That one friend who's always talking about how she's going to open up a spa one day and it will be one of the hottest spots in Atlanta. And you get excited for her every time she shares her vision of its candy apple red, black and white décor. But when you ask her when she's going to stop talking about it and just do it, she gives you some tired ass answer like, "I don't know girl. One day." You know the person I'm talking about. The one who gets so excited, but never puts that energy or excitement into making it happen for themselves! Or maybe YOU'RE that friend. Now, please understand there's nothing wrong with speaking life into your dreams. However, some people talk so much that they often confuse it for actively getting stuff done. Sometimes you've got to keep a tight lid on the dream. Silence allows the passion of your dreams to boil up, bubble over and absorb itself into every cell in your body. The result? Courageously and fearlessly moving toward the manifestation of what you want. Now tell me that isn't some fuel for your ass! Times when you feel like you want to keep shouting it out, write it down, put it in an envelope, set a deadline then get to work. Speak on it once and then let your passion do the rest.

What I mentioned above is exactly what I did when I got the vision to start Million Moms In Action (MMIA). I knew I wanted to start a movement, but I wasn't sure about how I was going to do it. I had this amazing vision for it but couldn't quite figure out the HOW. So I reached out to a friend of mind, Shannon Baylor-Henderson, and told her about the vision I had and how clueless I was at executing it. Besides the fact that we both are moms and business owners, we shared a lot in common and I valued her opinion greatly. After hearing me out, she said, "Well why don't you start a magazine?" And immediately it was like a light bulb went off and everything made sense. I said, "A magazine, oh my god that's perfect!" She went on to give me ideas about how to create the magazine because she'd done it previously for a few of her clients. I was bubbling with so much excitement that I could barely hold it in and I wanted to tell everyone. Instead, I decided not to reveal anything until I'd had a chance to put things together. I'd had absolutely no experience with magazines (other than reading them), but it all felt right and I immediately got to work. That night as I was working on creating content for the magazine, my husband walked in and asked what I was doing. I told him I was starting a magazine and shared my vision and my plan. He agreed it was a great idea and proceeded to offer advice on things to include. I thanked him and asked him to keep it between us because I didn't want anyone to know until the time was right.

Just 2 ½ months later, the first issue of MMIA (Million Moms in Action) magazine was born. I made the official announcement via social media, tagged all my family and friends and invited them to the launch party. Everyone was shocked that I pulled together the first issue after only two months because of the magnitude of the work involved and with very little help. But it was the fire, the passion, the vision that boiled in me and gave me the fuel to get it done.

Trick: Stop Waiting for Some Big Sign.

The time will never be right. There is no such thing as the perfect time or perfect weather. You're either going to do it or not! And if you're going to do it, then have faith you will succeed. We're so quick to ask for our prayers to be answered, but we're too slow to show God that we truly want it. You're so busy waiting on a sign that you didn't realize that YOU, my love, ARE the sign! Yes, you read that correctly, YOU are the sign. When you ask God, the Universe, Allah, Jehovah (or whatever higher power you speak to) for something, be prepared to show you're ready for it. And how you show you're ready for it is by taking a step out on faith. When you do that, you are signaling that you're ready and you're willing to walk the path necessary to achieve it. That signal is then answered in the form of a person, place, or thing and in the nature of an opportunity to move further ahead. Every step you take gives signals that you're ready for the next level, then God or the Universe leads you to another open door and another mind-blowing opportunity. Stay focused, keep your eyes open and everything you need will appear. Now how's that for a little magic?

"Life is very short and what we have to do must be done in the now."

–Audre Lorde

Chapter 3
No Queen Left Behind

There's this rumor going around about black women and we're going to put an end to it right now. You've either heard this rumor or you're guilty of spreading this yourself. The rumor is black women don't get along. They don't like each other and they're always fighting over something--a man, who looks better and other stupid shit. Now let's be real, some women are so lost and insecure that they don't know how to do anything but be petty, catty and vindictive. And what makes it worse is when people of other persuasions see this and assume that all women who look like this act out of character. But that is so far from the truth. What do you think happens when these same women step into a room filled with ambitious, loving and supportive women who speak nothing but life into each other? They get infected and eventually let their guard down. The woman begins to accept and merge into the energy that is present because it's overpowering and the love feels great. It's their natural way of being; it's in their nature. Energy is infectious. That's why it's so important to live out the same principals we teach our children. We say: Be nice. Don't make fun of people. Don't laugh at someone else's pain. Sometimes they may see us violate the same rules we just drilled into them just 20 minutes ago. We must be consistent with our actions by continuing to set the example of how to support and uplift each other.

Trick: Align Yourself with Those Who Share Common Goals & Values.

Get rid of negative Nancy and complaining Kim. Ain't nobody got time for that. I'm talking about women who always got "the tea" or stay busy trying to brew some up. You can't expect to flourish in a toxic atmosphere so why even entertain it? Instead, find a group of women who are ambitious and on the same path as you. Then invite the negative Nancys and complaining Kims. If they join you, then that's a clear sign they want and need more positive energy in their lives. But, if they decline, then allow them the much-needed space to figure things out for themselves. Once they see how much you've grown without them, they will likely make their way over. And for those who do not, continue to uplift them and send them positive energy and prayers.

Trick: Don't Compete, Support.

Whenever I see one of my sisters killing it in their career, home life, relationship, or whatever I smile and cheer for them. Their success reminds me that mine is just around the corner. Why be upset or jealous of what they have? Is their success negatively affecting your life? No! Those who react negatively do so because it illuminates the changes they need to make in their personal life. And because they have not made those changes they decide to diminish that light because it alleviates the pressure they feel to step things up in their lives.

    Having an encouraging group of friends who love,

support and inspire helps to keep you on your A-Game. Be each other's rock when you need it. Be the shoulder to lean on when needed. Be the sister she needs and vice-versa. When you work together, you win together. Network and get others like yourself involved. Collaborate and work together to build instead of competing. Sometimes you may have to go outside of familiar surroundings. You'll find that some of your biggest supporters are people outside of friends and family. Social media is great for connecting with like-minded people inside and outside of your community. Grind together and shine together!

Work Your Magic:

Jot down a list of at least five women (ten if you're up for the challenge) who share similar goals and values then reach out to them. Set up play dates and fun outings so you can build a sincere relationship of love and mutual support. Ask them to introduce you to the other women in their circle as well.

1._____
2._____
3._____
4._____
5._____
6._____
7._____
8._____
9._____
10._____

"It's not the load that breaks you down, it's the way you carry it."
\-Lena Horne

CHAPTER 4
BAG LADY TENDENCIES

Yes, as moms we have a lot on our plate, but I think we've used our roles as moms as crutches when it comes to getting shit done. Yes, it's true that often our children have situations that make it hard for us to move freely. However, it is equally true that we will use our children as an excuse to get out of doing something we don't want to do. And so I think it becomes convenient after a while for us to automatically use our children as an excuse whenever we're faced with challenges, especially, the scary or intimidating ones.

Years ago when I started growing my online health and beauty business, Green4Lyfe.com, I was a homeschooling mom who also worked from home. And although most women I know would kill to be a stay-at-home mom (or wife for that matter) it's A LOT of work and not easy. Not only did I have the everyday duties of cooking and cleaning but I also had the task of teaching my 1 and 3-year-old the basics of how to count, read and write, and trying to grow my business all on my own. I would complain about how I didn't have enough time to dedicate because the children and the house chores took up all of my time. I remember venting to my mom on the phone and she would say, "That's what being a mom is all about, Neoshi." But of course being the rebel that I am I would say to myself, shhhiiiit not ME! I became very frustrated and irritated so that I started purposely neglecting housework and instead worked on my business. And of course, my husband would come home and look at me like I was crazy and say, "Why in the hell does the house look like this?" My response was to get upset and immediately blame him for not helping out more with the cleaning around the house. Now mind you, this man was working 9-6 every day and paying ALL of our bills. Yes, he left things lying around like most men do but in no way should I have blamed anything on him. We both agreed to play certain positions in our home and he was most definitely playing his. The problem was I didn't know how to balance all of the roles I had to play.

Trick: Find Your Rhythm & Do What Works Best for You.

After a few weeks of arguing and blaming him, my husband sat me down and asked me this: "What do you need love? How can I help make things easier on you?" **Side note: Did I tell you I have the best husband in the world!?**

I swear it was at that moment that I realized I was making shit way too complicated. I was trying to live up to the ideal of what a "good mom" and "good wife" was supposed to be. Trying to wear the "supermom" cape that says I should be able to cook, clean, take care of the kids, work 8 hours a day, spend quality time with my husband and still have enough time to get 8 hours of sleep every night. But that's not realistic. That's crazy! And I was driving myself crazy trying to live up to standards made up by someone (society) I didn't even know. Not only was it draining, but I was also limiting and allowing myself to become a victim of society. What a moment of realization!

So, I told my husband that a sitter would help a lot even if it were just for a few hours a day. That way I would be able to knock out some work I needed to do for the business. He obliged and said, okay then let's find a sitter. And just like that, a weight was lifted off my shoulders. I no longer felt helpless but empowered and unstoppable. I gained 3 hours of uninterrupted grind time while the sitter attended to my babies. Each day when she arrived, I provided her with a list of activities I wanted them to do and asked her not to interrupt me unless it was necessary. I was relieved; I'd finally found my rhythm!

Finding your rhythm is about finding a way of life that works for you. It is a uniquely defined schedule that fits all the important aspects of your daily life. You know you've found it when your days run much smoother and your stress level is at a minimum. You'll be happier and your children will be happy too. Your rhythm allows you the freedom to move according to your personal lifestyle but may change depending on what you're working to achieve. It's never perfect, but it's always perfect for you.

Work Your Magic:

Jot down the most important tasks of your day (these are your non-negotiable; I must get it done, everyday tasks).

1._____
2._____
3._____
4._____
5._____
6._____
7._____
8._____
9._____
10._____

Once you've done that separate the list into two categories: "Assigned to Me" and "Re-assigned to Help". The tasks listed as "assigned to me " are tasks that <u>only you</u> can perform and includes things such as breastfeeding, work meetings and exercising. "Re-assigned to help" are tasks that can be handled by someone other than yourself such as your husband, friends and family, or older children. These include things such as preparing dinner, pick-up & drop-off the children, or washing/folding laundry. Having a support system is crucial to your success. Without it you can expect to get only so far.

Trick: Enlist Your Support System & Get Creative with Your Resources.

Your support system is often comprised of your spouse, close friends and family. They are the people who are aware of your goals and are willing to help you on your journey of getting there. Resources are tools and/or people who are available to help you solve a problem and/or point you in the right direction to solve your problem. Your job is a resource (pays your bills and can fund your new business). The next door neighbor who works at your dream job is a resource (can give you advice on do's and dont's). Often, people in your support system will also serve as a resource. And sometimes a resource becomes a part of your support system.

No one achieves anything of value without some help. But knowing how to use that help is what will get you closer to your goals. When you need an emergency sitter you know, you can count on grandma. When you need someone to proofread your work you know, you can count on your best friend. If you need an additional recommendation letter, you know your old college professor (who just happens to be chairman of the board) would be the perfect resource. However, be careful not to abuse your support system or resources so that you'll always have them when you need them most.

Work Your Magic:

Make a list of all the people in your support system. Then using the "Re-assigned to Help" list above, indicate how each one can assist you with your daily tasks.

Resource #1:_____
Task: _____
Resource #2:_____
Task: _____
Resource #3:_____
Task: _____
Resource #4:_____
Task: _____
Resource #5:_____
Task: _____
Resource #6:_____
Task: _____
Resource #7:_____
Task: _____
Resource #8:_____
Task: _____
Resource #9:_____
Task: _____
Resource #10:_____
Task: _____

"You are the designer of your destiny; you are the author of your story."

–Lisa Nichols

Chapter 5
Put Some Respect On It

We spend so much time daydreaming and so little time living. You watch Reality TV (aka Ratchet TV) but fail to realize that the only true reality is the one you create for yourself. So if your idea of reality is watching other people succeed and flourish, then that's exactly what your life becomes. There is nothing wrong with daydreaming though. It's useful and reminds you of your potential. But your potential is never achieved when you only dream. One of my favorite quotes I see a lot on social media says, "The dream is free, but the hustle is sold separately." I have no idea who said this, but that's not as important as the principle it brings to light. To get the life of your dreams, you've got to put in some serious work. It's not going to come from just posting a few ads online or watching a couple of motivational videos. You've got to get serious about developing a strategy to achieve it. And as with everything, nothing is manifested without first having a vision.

Trick: Set Goals Like a Pro!

I don't know about you, but it feels damn good when I can check things off a list. Like my daily to-do list. It makes me feel great that I'm actually accomplishing what I set out to do rather than feeling like I've been running around in circles all day. This is the same concept with goal setting. When you set a goal and reach it, it not only feels good but you accomplished what you wanted. Imagine if you achieved everything you wanted in life. When it was time for you to transition out of this world you left with no regrets and no woulda, shoulda, coulda. And based on experience (and statistics) you're more likely to go after a goal when you take it a step further and write it down. Writing it down takes it out of your head (daydreaming) and puts you one step closer to materialization.

Work Your Magic:
Jot down 5 (or more if you have them) short term and long term goals. Be very specific. Write them in a manner that you answer the questions what, how much, when, how, and how long. Example: Goal - Lose 10 pounds and 2 inches this month (Goal deadline: December 31, 2016). Jot them down no matter how silly, or out of the box, they may seem.

Short term goals (what you want to accomplish in 6-12 months):
1._____
2._____
3._____
4._____
5._____

Long term goals (what you want to accomplish in next 5, 10, 20 years)
1._____
2._____
3._____
4._____
5._____

This exercise will be a wake-up call once you've completed the list. You'll probably want to kick yourself for wasting so much time and you'll wish you started a long time ago. But, don't let the answers discourage you. Take it as a lesson and use it as the fuel to get you there. Imagine how great you will feel when you've looked back at your goals five years from now and have accomplished so much. That right there is priceless!

Trick: Create a Vision Board

I first learned of vision boards in my early 20's, but it wasn't until I met Lucinda Cross-Otiti, international vision board guru, that I realized the power of them. Lucinda's life is a prime example of how quickly your life can change when you know what you want. Mistakes made in her early college years landed her 4 ½ years in Federal Prison. But despite her tarnished record and lost time she manifested the career she wanted, the man she wanted and the life she wanted all because she had the audacity to dream it first. One of her recent dreams came true when she landed herself and her vision boards smack dab in the middle of Essence magazine which featured an article on her life and the power of vision boards. Lucinda is one of the hundreds of thousands of people who have used the power of visualization to create everything they've ever dreamed of and more. There is no hocus-pocus to it. It's all about knowing what you want, declaring it and making moves to make it happen. Vision boards keep you going when things get tough and are daily reminders of what you're working to accomplish.

I created my first vision board in 2013 (shown below). It was a declaration of the things I wanted most at that time in my life. That included a great education for both my children, advancement in my business, writing my first book (which you're reading right now), and so much more. As I write this, every single one of those things has either manifested or are in the works of becoming a reality. Vision boards are a powerful reminder that your life can become whatever you want it to be.

Work Your Magic:

Create your very own vision board using the supplies below:
- Poster board (as large as you'd like)
- Scissors
- Glue or tape
- Magazines (old or new)
- Markers, glitter, stickers (optional)
- Photos of yourself and family (if you want to go all out)
- A list of your dreams, goals, and ambitions

You can do this alone or with a group of friends. Carve out at least 3 hours, grab some drinks and snacks. Close your eyes and visualize the life you'd like to have, goals you'd like to achieve and how you'd like to feel. See it, smell it, touch it, taste it. You can focus on one specific area of your life, all areas of your life, or the year ahead. No goal is too big. No dream is unachievable. Don't listen to anyone who tells you it's a silly dream. After all, it's your dream, not theirs. Once you complete your vision board, hang it on a wall where you will see it every morning when you rise and every night before bedtime.

Trick: Create a Strategic Blueprint

Now that you know what you want, make a plan on how you're going to get it. So far you've written it down and envisioned it, but now you've got to plan it out. Vision boards are a start, but they won't get the job done. You need a strategic plan in place to help you get from point A to point B. That means planning monthly, weekly and daily tasks that when executed correctly will lead you directly to your goals.

"You don't make progress by standing on the sidelines, whimpering and complaining. You make progress by implementing ideas."
                                                    - Shirley Chisholm

Work Your Magic:

Choose two goals you want to focus on first. Break down each major goal into smaller monthly goals that you can accomplish one by one. Then break down your monthly goals into weekly goals. And finally, you spread your weekly goals across the entire week (assigning at least 1 task for each day of the week). Each daily goal (task) should lead you to the next step required to accomplish your major goal (see example below).

Goal #1: Dedicate the next six months to starting my own business and launch it on January 1, 2017

THE BLUEPRINT:
June 2016 Goals – Conduct background research on the industry and industry pitfalls via books, industry professionals, and potential clients/customers.

<u>Week 1 Goal(s) –</u> Reach out to people I know in the industry to get advice
- Task(s) for day 1 – Email old professor for coffee meeting
- Task(s) for day 2 – Call Marie and schedule meeting next week
- Task(s) for day 3 – Stop by Paul's office during lunch
- Task(s) for day 4 – Inbox Betty for lunch meeting
- Task(s) for day 5 – Search for Ke'Aundra's number and text her for drinks

- Task(s) for day 6 – Purchase a planner and exclusive notebook for biz
- Task(s) for day 7 – Write a list of questions for next week's meetings

<u>Week 2 Goals –</u> Attend all scheduled meetings and take extensive notes; get book recommendations
- Task(s) for day 1 – Meeting with Terri at 12 noon
- Task(s) for day 2 – Phone meeting with old professor at 10 am
- Task(s) for day 3 – Meet with Tommy at 3 pm
- Task(s) for day 4 – Have drinks with Ke'Aundra at 6 pm
- Task(s) for day 5 – Follow-up with old professor via phone
- Task(s) for day 6 – Review notes from meetings
- Task(s) for day 7 – Locate recommended books at bookstore and/or library

<u>Week 3 Goals –</u> Send 'Thank you' notes for meetings last week; Find and purchase/borrow books
- Task(s) for day 1 – Send thank you note to Terri, Tommy, Ke'Aundra, professor
- Task(s) for day 2 – Search for books in local bookstores
- Task(s) for day 3 – Call local library to see if books available
- Task(s) for day 4 – Pick-up books from library
- Task(s) for day 5 – Purchase books at local bookstore

- Task(s) for day 6 – Order last book online
- Task(s) for day 7 – Write a list of potential customers (names and #s)

<u>Week 4 Goals</u> – Call people I know who are potential customers/clients
- Task(s) for day 1 – Create a questionnaire for meetings
- Task(s) for day 2 – Call Alexis 8 pm
- Task(s) for day 3 – Call Fila at 4 pm
- Task(s) for day 4 – Call Ashley at 2:30 pm
- Task(s) for day 5 – Call Marsha at 5 pm
- Task(s) for day 6 – Call Nicole at 1 pm
- Task(s) for day 7 – Call Deborah at 9 am; Review notes from calls

July 2016 Goals- Choose 3 of 6 books from recommendations and read them entirely.

Week 1 Goals – Read book 1; Read at least 1 chapter a day
- Task(s) for day 1 – Read chapter 1
- Task(s) for day 2 – Read chapter 2
- Task(s) for day 3 – Read chapter 3-4
- Task(s) for day 4 – Read chapter 5
- Task(s) for day 5 – Read chapter 6-7
- Task(s) for day 6 – Read chapter 8-10
- Task(s) for day 7 – Read chapter 11-13

And so forth for every month after that, until your pre-set deadline. Now you may have to make revisions to your tasks as you go and that's okay. The important thing is you have an idea of what's next and start doing it. Make sure you plan to do something every day (even if it's just a simple phone call) to work towards one of your goals. Remember action is the name of the game if you want to win.

Trick: Execute, Slay, Repeat.

You've got your plan, and now it's time to WORK! And I mean give it everything you got. In the next two years you want to be able to look back on every single task and say, "YAAASSSSS, I DID THAT!" Giving a half-assed effort only returns half-assed results (if any at all). Execute every task as if it's THE most important task in the world. Non-coincidently, opportunities may arise when someone else witnesses your hard work and dedication. Their view of your work often leads you to connect with on-lookers who want to assist you in your endeavors. Valuable resources have been created this way and can be used to help you manifest other goals listed on your vision board. Remember these are your dreams you're going after. Do something every day that will count towards you achieving your goals.

Trick: Be Persistent; Focus on Solutions and Not the Problems

As with all goals, roadblocks and challenges are bound to surface. But when they do you will be well prepared for them if you remember this one jewel: Focus on solutions and not the problem itself. Don't talk yourself out of doing or changing your goal. Don't think about every stone that's been thrown your way. Don't sulk in frustration and start feeling sorry for yourself. Just clear everything off the table and ask yourself HOW can I make this happen? It's simple yet extremely powerful. If you're driving your car on a rocky road and the tire blows you don't get out and leave the car do you? No. You carefully pull over to the side of the road, change the tire and keep it moving. Battles are not won by concentrating solely on the wounded but by exploiting your enemy's weakest points.

"You are on the eve of a complete victory. You can't go wrong. The world is behind you."

–Josephine Baker

CHAPTER 6
CHICK DON'T KILL MY VIBE

You are a Goddess! At every second of the day, you are creating your reality. Even when you don't know you're creating, you are. Sometimes we blame other people for our circumstances, but the truth is its YOU who is in control. When you don't claim control of your life, you are allowing someone else to come in and call the shots. You might tell yourself you don't have a choice, but we both know that's not true. Deep down inside you know, you do! Telling yourself otherwise is like saying there's an up but no down. Ying, but no Yang. You always have a choice. If you're in a place you don't want to be, you have the choice to remain there or simply remove yourself. That's called 'Free Will.' To make every moment what you want it to be. Whether it's deeper love, more money or more me-time, you have the power to start creating it right now. And with that power comes responsibility, right? Which means making sure you are making healthy choices about your life and what you will allow into it. Think of this, the same as the responsibility you felt immediately after you found out you were pregnant with your first child. It was your duty to protect and shield that child from anything that might be harmful to him or her. So you stayed away from certain foods, took your prenatal pills regularly and avoided any strenuous activities. Your dreams are like babies too and they need to be protected and nourished in the same way. To see them grow from a vision to a living reality, you've got to proceed in the same manner as a mother would.

Trick: Protect the Energy of Your Space

Protecting your energy requires you to pay attention to the mental, physical and spiritual food you feed yourself. From the food you eat to the shows you watch and the thoughts you think. It's all connected! Protection also means being selective about what or who you allow in your space. Remember, the one thing you can't control is others and the energy they bring. Chemistry taught us that energy could not be destroyed or created but only transferred from one object to another. Which is why you can "feel the tension in the room" among people who are or were arguing. Everything is energy. And if the energy in your home or body is harmful in any way it can sabotage your results or the success you're after. So instead of watching the latest episode of Housewives, read a book written by someone who inspires you. If you like to scroll through social media, make sure you follow only those who are drama-free. Don't forget your physical body either. Meaning, making a real effort to adopt healthier eating choices as well. I know this is challenging to do especially when you're ripping and running all day. However, we both know that a healthy body is a happy body. When you take care of your body, it rewards you with things like more energy, fewer aches and pains and longevity.

Trick: Pray, Meditate & Ask for Guidance

Sometimes we get so caught up in this 9-5 driven world we forget we're here to do more than just pay bills and die. The disconnection is crippling and is partly why a lot of people leave this earth feeling unfulfilled, never reaching their full potential. When someone says 'life" got in the way of their dreams, what they're truly saying is that their connection to God or higher energy wasn't there or it was short lived. Whether you subscribe to prayer or meditation, we are all seeking to connect with a higher energy. It's the one thing that reassures us that we are here for a divine reason. The beauty of a divine connection is that it is unique to each of us. There is no right or wrong way to connect and neither is a certain way more superior. When connecting with God or your higher self, ask for guidance in your life and the path that will lead you to your higher purpose. Knowing your purpose is a game-changer. It's at that point when you realize that everything you've been dreaming of is a vision that was given to you by The Most High. It's that vision, your dreams; that connect you to your higher purpose. And it was gifted to you because you possess the unique qualities and passion for helping yourself carry it out in a way that only you can. So in everything you do, seek guidance and give thanks for the vision and responsibility that was gifted to you.

"It's time for you to move, realizing that the thing you are seeking is also seeking you."
– **Iyanla Vanzant**

Conclusion

By now you've realized just how magical you are; the kind of magic that doesn't require any mysterious spells, potions or mystical folklore. Simply put, it's the magic that comes from within. You see all of the "tricks" I shared with you speak to the essence of who you are. You are more than just a mother. You are more than just a woman. You are the epitome of creation. The fact that all of humanity came directly through you is all the proof you need. You are bigger than any battle you face and so are your dreams. No matter what situation you're presently in, know that you possess everything you need to change it at this very second. Be that example for your child(ren). Show them more than you tell them. By your example, teach them they can overcome all of their challenges and it's overcoming those challenges that will make them the person they want to be. Show them that life is a school of never ending lessons meant to propel us closer and closer to our higher purpose.

In moving forward, challenge your beliefs because they will dictate the life you create for yourself. When negative thoughts appear, get rid of them and replace them with positive ones that support your growth. Don't subscribe to some else's limitations, think for yourself and think outside of the box. If you're not sure where to start, just start where you are. Trust your intuition and let it be your guide. Talk less and bubble more; use your passion as fuel to get there. Don't wait for some big sign to get started. Remember you are the sign. Align yourself with people who "get it" and have the same desire to change their lives as well. Support each other instead of competing. Get creative with your resources and enlist your support system so you can find a rhythm that works best for you. Be intentional, set goals and create a strategic blueprint to get you there. Give 100% of yourself, so your results will reflect the effort you put in. When problems arrive, because they will, focus on the solutions instead of the problem itself. Protect your dreams by being mindful of the energy you allow into your mental, physical and spiritual space and never lose connection to your source. Regardless of your religion, pray, meditate and ask for guidance from God or your higher self.

The days of "do as I say, not as I do" are over. It is time to lead! Rise and be the woman you know you can be! It's time to remind the whole world of all the glory that comes with your Black Mom Magic!

Willing you love, prosperity, peace, happiness and everything your heart desires. Peace & love Queens!

Neoshi Green-Kebreau

"What God intended for you goes far beyond anything you can imagine."
—Oprah Winfrey

About the Author

Neoshi Green-Kebreau is the Chief Mom in Action at MillionMomsinAction.com and the author of *Black Mom Magic: How to Use What You Got to Get What You Want*. After quitting her job in 2010 to become a stay-at-home mom, Neoshi launched her first business, Green4Lyfe.com which grew into a profitable 6-figure business in just two years with clients throughout the U.S, Caribbean, Canada, and Europe. Named one of StartUp Nation's 2014 Top 100 Leading Moms in Business, awarded 2014 High Achiever Award by Ilyasah Al-Shabazz (activist and daughter of Malcolm X), featured in Yahoo Parenting, Huffington Post Live, Hot 105FM and many other media outlets, Neoshi is a happy wife and mom of 2. Not only is she walking in her purpose, but she encourages other visionary women to do the same, with boldness.

Contact the Author
www.millionmomsinaction.com
blackmommagicbook.com
On social media @neoshiyaki